How to Stay Married

Introduction to revised edition

More than forty years ago, I dined next to Godfrey Smith, the gloriously convivial editor of the *Sunday Times* Colour Magazine, and regaled him with tales about the screaming domestic chaos of my first months of marriage. I explained that because we made love all night and I spent all day, except for a scurrying shopping lunch, at the office, then rushed home to wash, iron, clean the flat, cook and eat supper, make love all night, go to the office – a pattern that was repeated until one died of exhaustion and our flat was so dirty I found a fungus growing under the sink.

On one occasion, I told Godfrey, my red silk scarf strayed into the washing machine at the launderette, so my husband Leo's shirts came out streaked like the dawn and he claimed he was the only member of the rugger fifteen with a rose-pink jockstrap. Our attempts at DIY were just as disastrous, as we stripped off the damp course in the drawing room, then found we'd papered our cat to the wall like the Canterville Ghost. Godfrey laughed a lot and commissioned a piece called 'A Young Wife's Tale', which appeared in the *Sunday Times* colour mag.

My poor mother was subsequently besieged by telephone calls from her friends: 'Darling, what's a jockstrap?'

Shortly after I had the miraculous break of a column in the *Sunday Times*, which lasted thirteen and a half years. At the same time a publishing friend asked me to write a little book called *How to Stay Married*.

I was so unbelievably flattered that even though I'd

only been married seven years, I said yes, and was soon merrily laying down the law on everything from sex on the honeymoon to setting up house, from in-laws to infidelity. With a deadline of three months, however, as well as my new weekly column to write, a six-month-old baby to look after and a newish house in Fulham to try to run, my poor neglected Leo got very short shrift and grumbled the book should be called *How to Get Divorced*.

He was, in fact, a huge help with the writing and, as can be seen by his photograph on the jacket, was the handsome hero of the book, which amazingly was published on time in October 1969 and even received some kind reviews.

Forty-two years later, when I blithely suggested reprinting *How to Stay Married* to coincide with our approaching golden wedding, my gallant publishers – to whom I have been happily hitched for almost as long – suggested I write a new foreword (or backward) from a fifty-year perspective. This entailed re-reading *How to Stay Married* for the first time since it was published, whereupon I nearly died of horror. What a smug, opinionated proselytising little know-all I was then. For a start, I announced sternly that men detested seeing women slaving in the house, so their wives must arrange to work from 8.30 a.m. to 4.30 p.m. so they could rush home and clean, iron and cook before their husband returned.

'If you amuse a man in bed,' I went on, 'he's not likely to bother about the mountain of dust underneath it,' or even more hubristically, 'be unlikely to stray.'

How could I have insisted that 'a woman should be grateful her husband wants her,' and suggested that if a wife refuses her husband sex then she has only herself to blame if he's unfaithful. Ouch, ouch!

Amending this bit is one of the only changes I have made to the text.

More shamingly, I have never practised what I preached, advocating total honesty about money being essential in marriage, and that 'couples should always know what the other is spending'. And that from a wife who regularly smuggled new clothes into her wardrobe, ripping off the price tag, lying: 'This old thing.'

'No wife has the right to go to seed,' I thundered, when I myself become a positive hayfield when I'm trying to finish a book, not washing my hair for days, hairy ankles sprouting out from ragged tracksuit bottoms. Yet not a word did I add urging husbands to exert self-control to avoid a beer belly.

Back in 1969, of course, men were expected to be masterful: 'If a man is married to a slut,' I pronounced fiercely, he must remonstrate with her, adding that 'women like a firm hand.'

'They'd probably prefer a farm hand,' observed Leo, when he read that bit.

My recommendations were all so dogmatic. One moment I was warning wives at the pain of divorce not to run out of toothpaste or loo paper, the next telling them how to detect if their husband was having an affair: 'If you both come home from work and the cat isn't hungry.' There was hardly anything about wives pursuing a career. If she needed a little money, I suggested, why not make paper flowers, or frame pictures?

Oh dear, oh dear. In mitigation, I suppose I was writing in a different age, when women's lib had hardly been heard of. No one had dreamed up New Men or paternity leave, and two-career marriages were a rarity, particularly if the couple had children. My own youthful ambition had been to marry a man

I'd fallen madly in love with, who'd whisk me away from the squalor of the typing pool. My role model was my beautiful mother, who looked after my father and us children so well because she never went out to work. My father, the breadwinner, because he called the shots, was surreptitiously nicknamed 'Monsieur Bossy' by my brother and me.

And yet despite the arrogance and the bossiness, I think there is good sense in much of *How to Stay Married*. What, I wonder, is the secret of a good marriage? Separate towns if you both snore, goes the old joke. Separate razors certainly. Today, probably separate remote controls.

My secret was to marry a really sweet man, who as I said back in 1969, had been married before. Thus after a cataclysmic row when I was tearfully packing my bags, he would reassure me that such tempests were normal in marriage and would blow over. Then he would make me laugh by saying we mustn't let Michael, our black cat, be the victim of a broken home.

Throughout our marriage he's constantly been funny.

'What does Jilly wear in bed?' asked one journalist, to which Leo replied, 'Dogs mostly,' and that when he reached over in the night for something furry, he would often get bitten.

Marriage, I've always believed, is kept alive by bedsprings creaking as much from helpless laughter as from sex. On our honeymoon we passed a large sign saying: 'Bear left for Norwich', and had this vision of some purposeful grizzly setting out on his travels. Soon the bear had spawned a whole family of other imaginary bears, about whom we made up silly private jokes and talked through them, as we always talk through our animals:

'You love that dog more than me,' Leo will say.

'I don't, I don't, he's just nicer to me sometimes.'

When we had been married forty years, in 2001, although reeling from the hammer blow of Leo being diagnosed with Parkinson's disease, we celebrated our ruby wedding with a very jolly party. In a speech, displaying far more humility than I ever did in *How to Stay Married*, I compared marriage to two people rowing across a vast ocean in a tiny boat, sometimes revelling in blue skies and lovely sunsets, sometimes rocked by storms so violent we'd nearly capsized, but somehow we'd battled on.

So many people gave us red or crimson roses, that we made a special ruby wedding flower bed in our garden. Ten years later as our golden wedding draws near, the roses are blooming, if a little battered, and the bed is invaded by wild flowers, happily including speedwell.

We have now reached a stage in our marriage when we worry much less about screwing than unscrewing the top on the Sancerre bottle or the glucosamine pills. We are utterly defeated by technology, but one of the plusses of six gorgeous grandchildren is they can turn on the DVD, use Google, send emails, change channels on wireless and television and record programmes for us.

Several hours a day are spent searching for credit cards, paper knives and spectacles, or a glass of wine left in an alcove in another room. The other day, we spent an acrimonious half-hour missing *Downton Abbey* as we searched frantically for the remote control, only to find Leo was sitting on it.

Having never mastered the metric system, I am utterly defeated by grams in cookery. Last week, as his red pair of cords plummeted to the floor, Leo announced he'd lost ten kilometres in weight.

Invitations and letters disappear in chucked-away newspapers, so people roll up unexpectedly for drinks or even dinner.

'You never told me they were coming.'

'I did, I did, but you never listen.'

But though domestic chaos is come again, I still believe that a happy marriage is the best thing life has to offer, cemented as much by the moments of irritation as of tenderness.

'For everyone, particularly children,' claimed Cecil King in 1969, 'the essential basis for security and happiness is a loving home.'

To counteract this, hideous recently released statistics reveal that 50 per cent of children today can expect their parents to split up by the time they are sixteen. More tellingly, a vast 80 per cent of these splits happen to unmarried couples. Marriage, for all its limitations, makes people try harder.

Children above all long for their parents to stay together. When a teacher asked one little girl to define love, she wistfully replied: 'Daddy and Mummy getting married.'

So I hope, despite some arrogance and smugness, that by charting the very real joys as well as the pitfalls – and panic stations – of our early years together, I may reassure and encourage more couples: married, unmarried, gay and straight, to stay together more happily.

God speed and good luck.

Jilly Cooper 2011

How to Stay Married

jilly cooper

drawings by Timothy Jaques

how to stay married

BANTAM PRESS

LONDON • TORONTO • SYDNEY • AUCKLAND • JOHANNESBURG

to Leo

contents

Introduction

It is extremely easy to get married – it costs £4.5s. and takes two days to get a licence. It is much harder to stay married.

My only qualifications for writing a book on the subject are that I have had the example of parents who have lived in harmony for nearly forty years, and I myself am still married extremely happily after eight years. In eight years, of course, we've had marvellous patches and patches so bad that they rocked our marriage to its foundations, but I've come to realise that if you can cling on like a barnacle during the bad patches, your marriage will survive and in all probability be strengthened.

Anyone else's marriage is a dark unexplored continent, and although I have observed far too many of my friends going swiftly in and out of wedlock, I can only guess at what it was that broke the marriage up, Since the word got around that I was writing this book, my task has been made doubly difficult by the fact that married couples either sidled away or started behaving ostentatiously well, whenever I came into the room.

One of the great comforts of my own marriage, however, has been that my husband was married before, knew the ropes, and during any really black period, when I was all for opting out and packing my bags, would reassure me that such black periods were to be expected in marriage, and it had been far worse for him the first time round.

Similarly I hope that by pointing out some of the disasters and problems that beset us and how we weathered them, it may reassure other people either married or contemplating marriage.

Here comes the bride

THE WEDDING

This is blast off – the day you (or rather your mother) have been waiting for all your life. It'll pass in a dream and afterwards you won't remember a thing about it. It helps, however, if you both turn up. Dope yourself with tranquillisers by all means, but watch the champagne later: drugs mixed with drink often put you out like a light. And don't forget to take the price tags off your new shoes, they'll show when you kneel down in church.

Brides: don't be disappointed if you don't look your best, far more likely you'll be scarlet in the face and piggy-eyed from lack of sleep.

Bride not looking her best

Bridegrooms: remember to look round and smile as your bride comes up the aisle. She'll be too busy coping with her bouquet and veil to notice, but it will impress those armies of guests lined up on either side of the church.

Groom smiling at bride

Coming down the aisle's more tricky – you never know where to look, that radiant smile can easily set into a rictus grin, and there's bound to be one guest you know too well, whose eye you want to avoid (like Tallulah Bankhead's remark about one couple coming down the aisle: 'I've had them both and they were lousy!').

If you look solemn, people will think you're having second thoughts. Best policy is to settle for a cool smirk with your eyes on the door of the church.

Be careful what hymns you choose. People like a good bellow at a wedding, so don't choose anything obscure. Equally, be careful of hymns with double meanings like 'Jesu – the very thought of thee', which will make everyone giggle and spoil the dignity and repose of the occasion.

THE RECEPTION

First there's the line-up, and you'll get so tired of shaking hands, trying to remember faces and gushing like an oil well, you'll begin to have a real sympathy with the Royal Family.

Don't worry when you circulate among the guests afterwards if none of them will speak to you. They'll all feel you're far too important to waste time talking to them, and you'll wander round like a couple of wraiths.

If you must make speeches, keep them short. Thank everyone in sight, and tell one stunning joke to convince your in-laws you do have a sense of humour after all. Never let the best man either speak or read the telegrams, unless he's very funny.

Don't flirt with exes. One girl I know, whose husband spent the reception playing 'do you remember' with an old girlfriend, refused to go on the honeymoon.

Try not to get drunk – you may feel like it – but it will cause recriminations later.

The honeymoon

Originally, the honeymoon was intended for husbands to initiate their innocent young brides into the delights and mysteries of sex. Today, when most couples have slept together anyway and are already bankrupted by the cost of setting up a house, the whole thing seems a bit of a farce and a needless expense. You probably both need a holiday, however.

When you arrive at your destination, you're likely to feel a sense of anti-climax. You're exhausted and suffering from post-champagne depression (a real killer). For months you've been coping with squabbles with the caterers, bridesmaids' tantrums over their head-dresses, parcels arriving every day, the hall littered with packing straw, writer's cramp from answering letters, traumas with the dressmakers – every moment's been occupied, you're wound up like a clock, and suddenly it's all over and you've nothing to do for a fortnight except each other.

For the wife in particular, everything's suddenly new and unfamiliar, her spongebag and flannel, new pigskin luggage, a whole trousseau of new clothes, dazzling white underwear instead of the usual dirty grey – even her name is new.

The thing to remember is that your wife/husband is probably as nervous and in need of reassurance as you are, like the wild beast surprised in the jungle who's always supposed to be more frightened than oneself.

SABOTEURS

The first thing to do on arrival at your honeymoon hotel is to search the bedroom for signs of sabotage. Jokey wedding guests may well have instructed the hotel staff to make you an apple pie bed, or wire up the springs of the bed to the hotel fire alarm.

One couple I know reached their hotel to be confronted by the manager waving a telegram from one such joker, saying: 'My wife has just run off with my best friend, I believe they are booked into your hotel under the assumed name of Mr and Mrs So and So. Could you refuse to let them have the booked room until I arrive?' Whether you're heading for the Bahamas or Billericay, the best way to scotch honeymoon saboteurs is not to be coy about your destination. Simply tell everyone you're staying at the Grand and then book rooms at the Majestic.

Then there's the problem of getting used to living together. Here again the wife in particular will be worried about keeping up appearances. Before marriage she's relied on mud packs and rollers and skinfood at night, but now her husband's going to be with her every moment of the day, and the mystery's going to be ruined. When's she going to find time to shave her legs? And she's always told her husband she's a natural blonde, and suddenly he's going to find the home-bleacher in her suitcase.

She'll soon get used to it all, just as she'll get used to sitting on the loo and gossiping to her husband while he's having a bath, or to wandering around with nothing on instead of discreetly changing in the bathroom.

If she's ashamed of her small breasts and mottled thighs, he's probably equally self-conscious about his narrow shoulders and hairless chest.

If she's ashamed . . .

FIRST THING IN THE MORNING

If you're worried you look like a road accident in the mornings, sleep with the curtains drawn, and if you're scared your mouth will taste like a parrot's cage when he bends over to kiss you, pretend you're going to the loo, and nip out and clean your teeth.

DON'T PANIC if you get bored, or have a row, or feel claustrophobic or homesick. These are all part of growing-together pains. They won't establish a behaviour pattern for the next fifty years.

A vital honeymoon ploy is to go somewhere where there is plenty to do. It's not sacrilege to go to the cinema or watch a soccer match or even look up friends in the district. Take lots of books and sleeping pills.

DON'T PANIC if you get on each other's nerves. My mother, who's been happily married to my father for over thirty years, nearly left him on honeymoon because he got a line of doggerel on his mind and repeated it over and over again as they motored through the cornfields of France.

We drove round Norfolk on our honeymoon and I nearly sent my husband insane by exclaiming: 'How lovely', every time we passed a village church.

SEX

I'm not going into the intricacies of sexual initiation – there are numerous books on the subject – I would just plead for both parties to be patient, tolerant, appreciative and understanding. Temporary frigidity and impotence are not infrequent occurrences on honeymoon, and not to be taken too seriously.

Take things slowly, you've probably got a lifetime in front of you – all that matters at this stage is to get across strongly that you love each other, and you're not sorry you are married.

DON'T WORRY if, unlike the girl in *The Carpetbaggers* who wanted to see nothing but ceilings on her honeymoon, you don't feel like leaping on each other all the time. As I've already pointed out, you're probably exhausted and in no condition for a sexual marathon.

Do take a red towel if you're a virgin, or likely to have the Curse. It saves embarrassment over the sheets.

Even if you've been sleeping together for ages beforehand, and sex was stunning, don't worry if it goes off for a bit, or feel convinced that it can only work in a clandestine setting. You haven't been married before, and may just be having initial panic because the stable door is well and truly bolted.

One friend told me he was woken up in the middle of most nights of his honeymoon by his wife staggering groggily out of bed, groping for her clothes and muttering she must get home before her parents woke up.

Eases tensions

It's a good idea to borrow someone's cottage in the country for a honeymoon. It's cheaper than a hotel, and you won't be worried by the imagined chortlings of chambermaids and hallporters, and you can cook if you get bored.

Don't worry if he/she doesn't gaze into your eyes all the time and quote poetry. Most people don't know enough poetry to last more than a quarter of an hour. A certain amount of alcohol is an excellent idea – it eases tension, breaks down inhibitions. Take the case of the girl in our office who on her arrival with her new husband at the hotel was presented with a bottle of champagne.

'It was wonderful,' she told us. 'We shared a glass each night and made the bottle last the whole fortnight.'

WEDDING PRESENTS

Get your thank-you letters written before the wedding. Once the pre-wedding momentum has been lost, you'll never get down to them.

Don't beef too much about the presents your partner's family or friends have given you, even if they are ghastly. No one likes to be reminded that they are related to, or acquainted with, people of execrable taste. Try and keep a list of who gave you what, so you can bring those cake forks out of hiding when Aunt Agatha comes to tea, and you won't, as we did, give a particularly hideous vase back to the woman who gave it to us, when later she got married.

Setting up house

MOVING IN

At best a nightmare – as Dorothy Parker said, the one dependable law of life is that everything is always worse than you thought it was going to be.

When my parents moved into their first house, they arrived to find the electricians had all the floor boards up, the paint was wet in the kitchen, and there was an enormous pile of rubble in the garage surmounted by a one-horned, one-eyed stag.

Try therefore to get all major structural alterations done beforehand. Nothing is more depressing than trying to get a place straight with builders trooping in and out with muddy feet and demands for endless cups of tea. Even the smallest job will seem as though they're building the pyramids.

Try to get shelves up beforehand; removal men unpack at a fantastic rate, and you'll soon find every inch of floor space covered and nowhere to put anything. Don't forget to get the gas and electricity connected. Buy plenty of light bulbs.

Make a plan where everything is going – or you'll end up with the grand piano in the lavatory, the fridge in the bedroom, and two little removal men buckling under the sideboard while you have a ferocious argument where to put it.

Get some food in. You'll be so busy, you won't realise it's past 5.30, and the shops are shut, and you'll be so bankrupted tipping the removal men and rushing out to buy picture wire, screws, and plugs, you won't have any money left to go out to dinner.

A bottle of whisky is an excellent soother of nerves – but don't let the removal men get their hands on it, or you'll have all your furniture chipped. A friend who had two particularly surly removal men made them a cup of tea and slipped two amphetamines into each mug. After that she had one of the jolliest moves imaginable.

How much to tip: about 10s a head – £1 if you're feeling affluent.

Do measure the height of the rooms before you go out and buy furniture in a sale. We had a tallboy standing in the street for weeks, because we couldn't get it through any of the doors.

If possible one of you should take a week off work (even if it is unpaid) to get things straight. Nothing is more demoralising than coming home late for the next month to face the chaos.

Try to get the kitchen and one other room habitable, then you can shut yourselves away from the debris when it becomes too much for you.

DO-IT-YOURSELF

One of the great myths of marriage – heavily fostered by television commercials of smiling young couples up ladders – is that home decorating is fun when you do it together.

It isn't. It's paralysingly boring and caused more rows in our marriage than anything else. Just remember that, like having a brace on your teeth as a child, it's worth it later on.

Invariably one partner is more hamfisted than the other, and the trouble starts when the more dexterous one becomes irritated and starts bossing poor Hamfisted about. Hamfisted gets more and more sulky until a row breaks out.

My husband is a great deal more adept than I am at decorating, but even so it was always a case of Wreck-it-Yourself. Our first attempts at wallpapering out-crazied the Crazy Gang. We lost our tempers, the measure and the scissors. I had bought enough paper

Our wrinkled, uneven labour

to do two rooms (wildly expensive at eight guineas a roll) but we had to scrap so much we only managed three quarters of one room. Finally, when we stood back to admire our wrinkled uneven labours, we found we had papered the cat to the wall like the Canterville Ghost.

A FEW POINTS TO REMEMBER
Buy cheap wallpaper for your first attempts.
When you strip wallpaper and come to a layer of silver paper, leave it alone, or you'll find you've stripped off the damp course, and any paper subsequently put on the wall will turn green.

PAINTING

Do remember to put dust sheets down when you're painting or you'll get shortsighted aunts commenting on the attractive speckled border round the walls.

If you're doing the landing and the hall, don't as we did start painting the landing scarlet, and the hall indigo – it never entered our heads that the colours would have to meet somewhere, in this case halfway up the stairs. The result is horrible.

Go to a showroom where you can see the paint you choose in large quantities. That colour that looks so subtle on the shade card can spread to vast deserts of ghastliness once it gets up on the wall.

Don't mix paints unless you're an expert: they always come out sickly ice-cream shades.

Never get friends to help. Even your own pathetic attempts will be better than theirs. We let a girlfriend, who claimed she found painting therapeutic, loose on one of the spare rooms. When we looked in a quarter of an hour later, there were terracotta flames of paint licking a foot high over the virgin white ceiling I had painted the day before. None of our cries of 'Steady on' or 'I say' could halt her. The whole room had to be painted again.

Tell your wife before you paint a shelf or she'll bustle in five minutes later and replace everything you removed. You are bound to have a row about who didn't wash the brushes last time.

If you run out of paint, do remember the name and brand before you chuck the tin away. We had to buy five different shades of orange before we hit on the right one again.

Lots of praise is essential. Say well done even if it isn't, people get inordinately proud of the four square foot of wall they've just painted.

MISCELLANEOUS

Curtains were another disaster zone – in an attempt to make them not too short, I made them miles too long, so they trailed on the floor like a child dressing up in its mother's clothes. And of course there wasn't enough material left over for the pelmets.

Don't be fooled by do-it-yourself tiling kits: they're easy enough until you have to round a corner or meet a natural hazard like a light switch.

TRADITIONAL ROLE OF HUSBAND AND WIFE

Traditionally the husband is the more practical and mechanically minded member of the partnership. But if he's the kind who hits the electricity main every time he knocks a nail in and puts up shelves at 10°, and his wife is the practical type who got a distinction for carpentry at school, she shouldn't hesitate to take over. As my husband remarked, here was one sphere in which he wouldn't have minded having his masculinity undermined.

Running the house

HOUSEKEEPING

A major problem for the newly married wife, particularly if she is holding down a nine-to-five job. Before she was married she blued her wages on clothes and took her washing home to Mother every weekend. Now, suddenly, she must be housekeeper, cook, hostess, laundress, seamstress, beguiling companion, glamour girl, assistant breadwinner and willing bedfellow all in one.

What she must remember when she gets home exhausted from the office to be faced with a mountain of washing up in the sink, the dinner to be cooked, the bed to be made, the flat to be cleaned, a pile of shirts to be ironed, and her husband in a playful mood, is that where marriage is concerned, CHEERFULNESS, SEXUAL ENTHUSIASM, AND GOOD COOKING are far nearer to Godliness than cleanliness about the house.

As long as the flat is kept tidy – men hate living in a muddle – meals are regular, and their wives are in good spirits, husbands won't notice a few cobwebs.

If you amuse a man in bed, he's not likely to bother about the mountain of dust underneath it.

RESENTMENT

If a wife feels resentful that she is slaving away, while her husband comes home and flops down in front of the television until dinner is ready, she must remember that it isn't all roses for him either.

He has given up his much prized bachelor status for marriage and he probably expects, like his father before him, to come home every night to a gleaming home, a happy wife, and a delicious dinner. Instead he finds a tearful, fractious shrew, and he forgets that his mother looked after his father so well because she didn't have to go out to work.

TOLERANCE

Tolerance is essential on both sides. If the wife is working, the husband must be prepared to give her a hand. Equally, it's up to the wife to ask when she needs help, and not scurry round with set face like someone out of *Foxe's Book of Martyrs*. As men hate seeing their wives slaving, one of the solutions is for the wife to get her housework done when her husband isn't around.

That housekeeping whizz-kid Mrs Beeton suggests getting up early, and I managed to persuade most of my employers to let me work from eight-thirty to four-thirty. Eight-thirty sounds horrendous, but once you're used to it, it's much the same as nine-thirty. You miss the rush-hour traffic both ways, you have a nice quiet hour in the office before anyone else gets in to ring your mother or make a shopping list (no one knows whether you got in exactly at eight-thirty anyway) and you get home at least an hour before your husband so you have time to get the dinner on, tidy up and welcome him home.

Another solution is to encourage your husband to have at least one night out a week with the boys, then you have a few hours to catch up.

DAILY WOMEN

Or you can employ a daily woman. If you get a good one, hang on to her, she's worth her weight in bullion. Generally, alas, dailies start off marvellously and then after a few weeks the standard goes down and so does the level of the gin. My husband came home once and found ours asleep in our bed with the electric blanket and the wireless on.

Asleep in our bed

If I have a good daily, I find I spend far more time than before tidying up before she comes, and if I get a bad one, I spend hours tidying up after her, so my husband won't grumble about throwing money away and force me to sack her.

Dailies also have an irritating habit of not turning up the day your mother-in-law is coming to stay, or the time you're relying on them to tidy up before a large dinner party.

But to return to housework. Remember that the dust you flick away today will have drifted back into place tomorrow. Once when I was rabbitting on about the dirtiness of my house, a girlfriend, whose house is none too clean either, told me I was suffering from the bourgeois syndrome: namely, obsessive worrying over spit and polish. It worked like a charm. I didn't do any housework for at least a fortnight.

A FEW QUICK POINTERS
Have lots of cushions to hide things under when guests arrive, and plump them a great deal. The woman who

Huge arm muscles

has the tidiest house in London has huge arm muscles from plumping.

Closing untidy desks, straightening papers, putting books back vertically instead of horizontally and records back in their sleeves, picking things off the floor: all make a room look better quicker than dusting or hoovering.

Empty ashtrays, clear dirty glasses into the kitchen, open windows at night, or the place will smell like a bar parlour in the morning.

Get a decent hoover, or you'll be like a girlfriend who grumbled to her husband that she was quite exhausted from hoovering all day.

He looked around and said: 'I wish you'd do some hoovering in our house instead then.'

Don't hoover under his feet – it's grounds for divorce. If your kitchen is a pigsty, don't have a glass door, or a hatch through which inquisitive guests can peer.

Don't use all the dusters for polishing silver or shoes, of you'll have to hare round before dinner parties dusting furniture with the front of your dress like I do.

LAUNDRY

If you can possibly afford it during the first six months, send your husband's shirts to the laundry; one of the things that nearly broke my back when I was first married was washing and ironing seven shirts a week. Do encourage your husband to buy dark shirts for the office, so he can wear them for at least two days.

If you wash at home, don't, as I always do, put in far too much soap powder and spend the next two hours rinsing.

If you wash at the launderette, remember to put your half-crown into the machine, or you'll come back forty minutes later to find your clothes still unwashed. Be careful not to put anything that runs into the machine. When we were first married I left in a red silk handkerchief. My husband's shirts came out streaked like the dawn, he wore cyclamen underpants for weeks and claimed he was the only member of his rugger fifteen with a rose pink jockstrap.

If you have a spin dryer, remember to put a bowl under the waste pipe or you'll have the kitchen awash every time. Drying is a problem in a small flat: one of the most useful presents we had was a Hawkins Hi-Dri (cost about £9), which will dry all your washing in about six hours and can be folded away afterwards.

Husbands are not amused by singe marks. They can be removed with peroxide, and in an emergency use talcum powder. Always put ironing away when you've finished – either the cat is bound to come and sit on it, or it looks so badly ironed it gets mistaken for dirty laundry and washed again.

The ideal, of course, is to send everything to the laundry. Unfortunately our laundry is notorious for not getting things back on time (we've got very used to the rough male kiss of blankets) and for 'losing' things.

CLEANING
Try to keep all cleaning tickets in one place. We always lose them, and at this moment, half our wardrobe is sitting in various cleaners all over London, soon no doubt to be sold second-hand.

FOOD
I got the sack from my first job after I was married because I spent all morning on the telephone apologising to my husband for the row we'd had on the bus, and all afternoon reading recipe books.

Cooking well and cooking cheaply is a major problem for the young wife. Before she was married she probably invited her fiancé to dinner from time to time and blued half her wages on double cream and brandy to go with the fillet steak and the shellfish, so that he is under the illusion that she is a marvellous cook. Now she is married she will find cooking exciting meals every evening and not overtaxing her imagination and the family budget extremely difficult.

Don't, however, be seduced into buying things that are cheap if they repel you. I once bought a black pudding, because I was told it was inexpensive and nourishing. It lay like a long black slug in the fridge for three weeks, finally turned green, died and was committed to the dustbin.

Ring the changes: however much he raves over your fish pie, he won't want it twice a week for the next fifty years.

Buy in bulk if you and your husband have self-control: we find bulk buying never does anything but increase our bulk. The joint that is bought on Saturday never graduates into cold meat and later shepherd's pie. It is always wolfed in one sitting. Once we made a big casserole to last a week. It took eight hours to cook, stank the whole block of flats out, and went bad the following day.

Buy in bulk

Leave long-cooking dishes to the weekend. Nothing irks a man more than having to wait until midnight to eat. Do take the stew off the gas before you start making love.

Never hide things – you won't remember where you put them. I hid some potted shrimps once and discovered them a month later after we'd had the floor boards up.

HUSBANDS

If you find a half bottle of wine in the kitchen, check before you drink it. Your wife may be saving it for cooking some exotic dish.

Don't be bossy in the kitchen. Nothing irritates a woman more than to be told to add some more paprika, or that your mother always made it with real mashed potato.

MONEY

Honesty about money is absolutely essential in marriage. If you are to avoid major rows, you must know how much money you've got in the bank, and how much each of you is spending.

In theory all bills should be kept together and paid at the end of each month. Weekly accounts should be kept and the financial situation should be reviewed every month.

In practice we never did any of these things. We both got married with overdrafts well into three figures – having lived at home I had no idea of the cost of living, and between us we were earning far less than £2,000 a year. We ricocheted from one financial crisis to another.

Economising is particularly hard when you're first married, for there are so many things to do to the house, and if the wife is determined to impress the husband with her cooking, it's cream and wine in everything.

We used to have absurd economy campaigns: drinking tea instead of coffee for breakfast, driving miles to find a garage which sold cheaper petrol, turning out the lights and creeping round in the dark to save electricity, smoking less (which meant we ate more), eating less (which meant we smoked more).

We did evolve a splendid bill-paying evasion technique.

We never paid a thing until we got a solicitor's letter; then we would send the creditor a cheque, unsigned, so they would spend another week returning it, whereupon it would be returned in successive weeks, with the date left off, the wrong year, or the numbers and letters differing.

Another ruse was to ring up when the final reminder turned up and say in aggrieved tones: 'But I've already paid it', and they'll spend at least a month trying to trace it.

With electricity, gas and telephone, you can always write and query the amount, saying you've been away for the last month and you can't think why the bill is so high.

Perhaps the best method is to keep sending the bill back with 'Not known here' written across it.

I tried once to keep accounts and in the third week, when I was making great efforts to economise, I saw to my horror that the expenditure had doubled. I went sobbing to my husband, who pointed out quite kindly that I'd added the date in.

Try to pay the rates by the month – and why not investigate a household budget account with your bank manager? It considerably simplifies bill-paying. Another minor money problem is that one always assumes that one's partner will have some money on him, and he never has, so you find you have to jump off buses because neither of you can pay the fare, or walk home five miles from parties in the middle of the night because you can't afford a taxi.

Remember that each partner is bound to think the other one is extravagant, and that everyone always thinks he is broke however rich he is. As one friend said the other day: 'We're just as poor as when we were first married but on a grander scale.'

SHOPPING

Shop early in the morning when there's more choice, and mid-week when things are cheaper.

Always make a list, or you'll have the absurd situation of trailing miles to Soho market in your lunch hour, then buying all the things you've forgotten on the way home – at Fortnums.

Don't let men go near the shops, they'll blue the week's housekeeping on salmon and rump steak and come home very smug because they've shopped so much more quickly than you would have done.

Take things out of your shopping bag and put them away at once, or you'll have frozen raspberries melting on to the drawing room carpet, and liver blood permanently on your cheque book.

Despite the maxim: 'If you can get it on tick it's free, if you can pay by cheque it's almost free, but if you have to pay cash, it's bloody expensive,' pay cash if you can. Our biggest shopping bill is always drink, because we can chalk it up at the off-licence round the corner.

Be tolerant of each other's extravagances. Everyone lapses from time to time. One of the nicest things about my husband is that he never grumbles about my buying a new dress unless he thinks it is ugly.

TIDINESS AND UNTIDINESS

If the husband is married to a real slut, who constantly keeps the house in a mess and serves up vile food, he has every right to complain. There's a happy medium between being a doormat and a bully. Rather than work yourself into a frenzy of resentment, first try to tease your wife out of her sloppiness, and if that doesn't work, risk a scene by telling her it just isn't good enough.

A firm hand

Women on the whole quite like a firm hand, and one of the saddest things a wife ever said to me was: 'It was only on the day he left me that he told me for the first time that I was a lousy cook, I turned the place into a pigsty, I never ironed his shirts, and left mustard under the plates.'

Men like a place they can relax in and if the wife is the tidy one, she shouldn't nag and fuss her husband the moment he gets home.

'I can't stand it any longer,' said one newly married husband, 'she's taken all my books and put them in drawers like my shirts.'

'Among some of the best marriages,' my tame psychiatrist told me, 'are those in which, although the husband and wife started at relatively distant poles of neatness and sloppiness, they moved towards a common middle ground, through love, understanding and willingness to understand each other's needs.'

'If there's one thing I can't stand . . .'

CHANGING PEOPLE

You shouldn't go into marriage expecting to change people. Once a bumbler always a bumbler, once a rake always a rake (a gay eye isn't likely to be doused by marriage). Once a slut – although she may make heroic and semi-successful attempts to improve – always a slut. When we were first married, my husband used to dream of the day I stopped work, like the Three Sisters yearning for Moscow: 'The house will be tidy, we shall make love every morning, and at last I shall be given breakfast.'

Well, I stopped work, and chaos reigned very much as usual. It's a case of *plus ça change*, I'm afraid.

Your only hope is that by making people happier and more secure they may realise the potential inside them and develop into brilliant businessmen, marvellous lovers, superb cooks, or alas, even bores. And remember, the wife who nags her husband on to making a fortune won't see nearly so much of him. He'll be in the office from morn until night. She can't have it both ways.

DIFFERING TASTES

Certain things are bound to grate. He may have a passion for flying ducks and Peter Scott and she may go a bundle on coloured plastic bulrushes and a chiming doorbell.

The wife may also use certain expressions like 'Pleased to meet you,' which irritate her husband to death; or he may say 'What a generous portion' every time she puts his food in front of him.

Now is the time to strike. If you say you can't stand something in the first flush of love, your partner probably won't mind and will do something about it. If, after ten years, you suddenly tell your husband it drives you mad every time he says: 'Sit ye down' when guests arrive, he'll be deeply offended, and ask you why you didn't complain before.

IRRITATING HABITS

Everyone has some irritating habits – the only thing to do when your partner draws your attention to them is to swallow your pride and be grateful, because they may well have been irritating everyone else as well.

I have given up smoking and eating apples in bed, or cooking in my fur coat, and I try not to drench the butter dish with marmalade. My husband no longer spends a quarter of an hour each morning clearing the frog out of his throat, and if he still picks his nose, he does it behind a newspaper.

There are bound to be areas in your marriage where you are diametrically opposed. Compromise is the only answer. I'm cold blooded, my husband is hot blooded. I sleep with six blankets, he sleeps half out of the bed.

I like arriving late for parties so I can make an entrance, he likes arriving on the dot because he hates missing valuable drinking time. I can't count the number of quiet cigarettes we've had in the car, waiting for a decent time to arrive.

Don't worry too much that habits which irritate you now will get more and more on your nerves. My tame psychiatrist again told me: 'Those quirks in one's marriage partner which annoy one in early days often become in later years the most lovable traits.'

Rows

My husband and I quarrel very seldom, we both loathe rows and hate being shouted at. I was very worried when I first married because I read that quarrelling was one of the most common methods of relieving tensions in marriage, and was confronted with the awful possibility that our marriage had no proper tensions.

It is very hard to generalise about rows. Some of the happiest married people I know have the most blazing rows, and then make it up very quickly – like MPs who argue heatedly in the House all night, and then meet on terms of utter amicability in the bar five minutes later.

However much a row clears the air, one is bound during its course to say something vicious and hurtful, which may well be absorbed and brooded upon later. Try therefore to cut rowing down to the minimum. It will upset children when they come along, and if you row in public, it's boring and embarrassing for other people, and you won't get asked out any more.

We found the occasions when rows were most likely to break out were:

Friday night – both partners are tired at the end of the week.

Going away for weekends – one person is always ready and anxious to avoid the rush-hour, the other is frantically packing all the wrong things, so the first five miles of the journey will be punctuated with cries of 'Oh God' and U-turns against the ever-increasing traffic to collect something forgotten.

Weddings – the vicar's pep-talk in church on Christian behaviour in marriage always sets us off on the wrong foot. Then afterwards we'll be suffering from post-champagne gloom and wondering if we're as happy as the couple who've just got married.

Television – husband always wants to watch boxing, and the wife the play.

Desks – the tidy one will be irritated because the untidy one is always rifling the desk, and pinching all the stamps and envelopes.

Clothes – men not having a clean shirt, or clean underpants to wear in the morning.

Space in the bedroom – the wife will appropriate five and three-quarters out of six of the drawers and three out of four of the coat hangers, and leave her clothes all over the only chair.

MINOR IRRITATIONS
ALL LIKELY TO CAUSE ROWS
The wife should avoid using her husband's razor on her legs and not washing it out, or cleaning the bath with his flannel, or using a chisel as a screwdriver, or pinching the husband's sweaters. There are also the eighteen odd socks in her husband's top drawer, the rings of lipstick on his best handkerchief, running out of toothpaste, loo paper, soap. Forgetting to turn out lights, fires, the oven. Forgetting to give her husband his letters or telephone messages.

MAKING UP
Never be too proud to apologise, but do it properly, none of that 'I've said I'm sorry, haven't I?', followed by a stream of abuse.

Don't worry about letting the sun go down on your wrath – it's no good worrying a row to its logical conclusion when you're both tired and then lying awake the rest of the night. Take a sleeping pill, get a good night's sleep and you'll probably have forgotten you ever had a row by morning.

Try not to harbour grudges, never send someone to Coventry.

A sense of humour is all-important for ending rows. My husband once in a rare mid-row put both feet into one leg of his underpants and fell over, I went into peals of laughter and the row was at an end.

Once when I was threatening to leave him he looked reproachfully at the cat, and said: 'But we can't let poor Michael be the victim of a broken home.'

Poor Michael

A note on feminine problems

BLACK GLOOMS

Suffered particularly by wives in the first six months after marriage, they usually stem from exhaustion, feeling totally unable to cope, and reaction after the wedding. They are extremely tedious for the husband, but nothing really to worry about unless they linger on longer than a week. Nothing will be achieved by telling her sharply to snap out of it – patience, a lot of loving and encouragement are the only answer.

THE CURSE

Should be re-named the blessing. Every row two weeks before it arrives, and a week after it's finished, can be blamed on it.

ANNIVERSARIES

Husbands are notorious for forgetting birthdays and anniversaries. Don't expect a heart-shaped box of chocolates on Valentine's Day, but avoid a row on the birthday/anniversary by saying loudly about three days before: 'What shall we do on my birthday/our anniversary on *Friday*, darling?'

Christmas

The row usually starts about September and continues through to February.

Wife: Where shall we go for Christmas, darling?

Husband: Anywhere you like, darling.

Wife: Well I thought we might spend a few days with Mother.

Husband (appalled): With your mother! No drink,

and frost because we don't go to church three times a day. If you think I'm staying with that old cow . . .

Wife (interrupting with some asperity): What did you have in mind?

Husband: Well I rather thought we might go to Scotland.

Wife: To stay with your parents! No central heating, and those damned dogs – that's charming.

And the row follows its normal course.

Many people like to go to their families for Christmas and they can't understand why their partners find it such a strain. If you can't stand going to either set of parents, get a large dog and say you can't leave it.

CHRISTMAS PRESENTS
These can be an awful bore, particularly if you come from large families. We've evolved a system whereby my husband buys all the men's presents, and I look after the women and children.

Relations and friends

IN-LAWS
The ideal is to marry an orphan. However hard you try, you'll probably have some trouble with your in-laws. Mine have always been angelic to me but as my mother-in-law pointed out to me in a moment of candour, nobody is ever good enough to marry one's children.

Be kind to your in-laws. Remember that many parents are so involved with their children that it's an act of infidelity almost tantamount to divorce when they suddenly meet someone and marry them. For years a

41

mother has considered herself her daughter's or her son's best friend, and suddenly she isn't. She sees them confiding in someone else, and as they draw further and further away from her, she becomes more and more unpleasant by trying to hang on to them.

Tact is essential. Be particularly nice to your husband/ wife when in-laws are around, but don't neck and don't exclude them with private jokes. From the wife a bit of sucking up doesn't come amiss. Ask your mother-in-law's advice about cooking and washing, say your husband is always raving about her apple pie, how does she make it?

One thing that particularly upsets mothers-in-law is heavy eye make-up and long untidy hair, so if you want to take the business of getting on with her seriously, tie your hair back and soft pedal the make-up when you see her.

The husband's best tack is to flirt with his mother-in-law, even if she's an old boot. Few women can resist flattery.

Wives can flirt with their fathers-in-law, but don't overdo it, or you'll have your mother-in-law branding you a fast piece.

However much you dislike having your in-laws to stay, be philosophical about it: at least it will make you clean the place up. My mother-in-law once slept peacefully and unknowingly on a pillow-case full of wet washing. Don't give them too lush food or they'll think you're being extravagant. Herrings and cider will impress them far more than lobster and caviar. And hide those battalions of empties before they arrive.

My husband always takes his parents on a tour of the house, pointing out things that need repairing in anticipation of a fat cheque.

YOUR OWN PARENTS

However fond you are of your own parents, remember that when a man marries 'he shall leave his father and mother and cleave unto his wife'.

Loyalty to your husband or wife must always come first. Don't chatter to your mother too long or too often on the telephone, it will irritate your husband and possibly make him jealous.

If you have a row with your husband or wife, and pack your bags, go to a discreet friend, never, never go home to your parents. You will say a lot of adverse things about your partner in the heat of the moment which you will forget afterwards, but your parents will remember them and it will be extremely difficult afterwards for your parents and partner to pick up the threads again.

FRIENDS

A friend married is a friend lost, goes the proverb, and certainly one of the sad facts of marriage is that it's almost impossible to keep up with friends one's other half doesn't like. You can relegate them to lunch dates and evenings when your partner is out, but invariably they get the message and sweep off in low-gear dudgeon.

Much of the first year of marriage is spent weeding out the sheep from the goats. Both parties should try not to be jealous of the other half's close friends. My husband certainly made short work of any friends he considered a) boring, b) unstable influences.

If you find your husband's friends a bore, establish a reputation for delicacy early on in the marriage, then when they lurch in drunkenly from the pub, you can plead exhaustion and disappear upstairs to read a book.

DROPPERS-IN

Ought to be abolished. People should telephone first and see if you want to see them. No one will bother you the first month or so. They used to apologise to us for telephoning after seven o'clock, assuming we'd be in bed. After that they'll descend in droves, looking curiously for signs of strain in your faces, avid to see what kind of mess you've made of your flat.

One method of getting rid of them is to dispatch your husband to the bedroom, rip off all your clothes, ruffle your hair, and, clad only in a face towel, answer the door brandishing the *Kama Sutra*. The droppers-in will be so embarrassed that they'll apologise and make themselves scarce.

Answering the door

Entertaining notions

ENTERTAINING

Always check with your partner before you issue or accept an invitation, or you'll get ghastly instances of double dating.

Time and again recently, we've been making tracks for bed when the telephone goes, and an irate voice says, 'Aren't you coming, we're all waiting to go in to dinner.' Or we'll be just leaving the house to go out, when a rosy-cheeked couple arrive on the doorstep having driven fifty miles up from the country for dinner.

Keep a book by the telephone and write everything down.

DINNER PARTIES

Unless you're a Cordon Bleu cook, and totally unflappable, your first dinner parties are bound to be packed with incident. Overcooked meat, undercooked potato salad, soufflés that don't rise, guests that don't rise to the occasion.

If you're a beginner, cook as much as possible the day before. Cod's roe pâté, liver pâté, soup, casseroles and most puddings can all be made beforehand. Then all you have to do the following day is to make the toast and mix a salad dressing.

If possible get the table ready the night before as well.

Polishing glasses, ironing napkins, getting out plates and coffee cups all take longer than one would imagine. Get plenty of cheese, in case you haven't given people enough – I once fell up the stairs with the pudding and eight plates, and there was no cheese in the house.

Guests

Don't spend hours away from your guests. Nothing is less calculated to put them at their ease than a hostess who turns up red in the face after three-quarters of an hour, grabs a quick drink and disappears again.

One couple we went to dinner with both disappeared for an hour to peel grapes for the Sole Véronique, and the whole meal was served to an accompaniment of piped cream.

Be careful who you ask with whom: the day our vicar's wife came to dinner we invited a young man who regaled us for half the evening with details of the mating habits of the rhinoceros.

Don't become a slave to social ping-pong. Entertaining is wildly expensive and just because you had caviar and three kinds of wine at the Thrust-Pointers, don't feel you have to give them oysters and liqueurs when they come back to you.

If you're broke, warn people beforehand that it will only be spaghetti and Spanish Burgundy, then they can either refuse, bring a bottle or have a number of stiff drinks beforehand.

If you're worried about the food, drink for at least an hour and half before you eat, and they'll be so tight they won't know what they're eating.

Equally, if you're supremely confident about your food, don't let them drink too much.

Don't play loud background music before dinner, it kills conversation. People can go to a concert if they want that sort of thing.

Never, never show slides.

IF THEY WON'T GO
The husband should make the first move by saying his wife is tired and sending her to bed. If that doesn't work, turn the central heating off.

If you don't like certain people, don't feel you have to ask them back. They'll get the message eventually. Life is too short to bother with people you really don't care for. You'll work up too much angst beforehand about having to see them, and too much spleen afterwards about how bored you were.

PARTIES
Make a list and stick to it. We always ask indiscriminately and have far too many people, both of us trying to smuggle in people the other doesn't like.

Don't send out invitations. You can't ask everyone, and people get very sour if they see your invitations on other people's mantelpieces. Also, if you invite by telephone, you get a 'yes' or 'no' immediately, and people are notoriously bad at answering letters.

We once gave a drears' sherry party – with fatal consequences. All our undreary friends found out and were furious they hadn't been invited, and the drears discovered why they'd been asked, and were deeply offended. We were a bit short of friends that year.

One of the secrets of a good party is a few abrasive elements. Recently we went to an outstandingly successful 'bring-an-enemy' party.

Don't expect to enjoy your own parties, except in retrospect. All your guests will be too busy getting drunk and trying to make other guests to bother about you. Your function is to act as unpaid waiter and waitress: effecting introductions, rescuing people whose eyes are beginning to glaze whether they're bored or drunk, and watching people's drinks.

Do mix a cocktail that can be poured, or give them wine, otherwise you'll get in a terrible muddle remembering what everyone wants and start giving them whisky and tonic and gin and soda.

GOING TO PARTIES

Don't stand together all evening, it will upset your hostess. Check every twenty minutes to ensure your partner isn't standing alone, doesn't need rescuing from the local bore, isn't pinned to the wall by the local sex maniac.

If you want to dance cheek to cheek with the most attractive man/woman in the room, wait until your husband/wife is securely trapped on the sofa in another room.

If you catch your partner making a pass at someone, smile broadly as though it was an everyday occurrence, say, 'Drink always takes him/her this way, he/she won't remember a thing about it next morning,' and whisk him/her away smartly.

HOW TO LEAVE

There is bound to be a moment when you want to go home and your husband doesn't because he's having too good a time, or vice versa. One of you will just have to grin and bear it. Don't get into the habit of leaving independently, it looks bad, and is very expensive on taxis.

Overcome with lust

If you're both bored, intimate to your hostess that you've been overcome by lust and must leave. She will think her party has been a contributing factor and be delighted, particularly if you leave murmuring about the seductive atmosphere.

The office

OFFICE PARTIES

If husbands and wives aren't invited, be extremely careful. This is the moment when Mr Chalcott in Accounts, who has been eyeing Mrs Pointer in Personnel all the year, suddenly gets too much drink in him, makes a pass at her and the whole thing erupts into an affaire. Try not to get home too late, be careful to wipe lipstick off your cheek if you're a man, and replace your make-up carefully if you're a woman. The fact that Mr Prideau in Packaging saw fit to pounce on you may be just Christmas high spirits, but it will worry your husband, who'll think it is normal procedure for the rest of the year.

If you go to your wife's or husband's office party, be

as nice as possible to everyone. These people may seem draggy to you, but your partner's got to put up with them all the year round, and will get tremendous kudos if you're a success.

Be prepared for anything – my mother went to my father's office party once when he was in a very senior position. She was hotly pursued by a man from the boiler division in a Mickey Mouse mask, who kept tracking her down in the Paul Jones, tossing her up in the air, and crying, 'I am your demon lover.'

Hotly pursued

Be careful what you wear, look pretty but not out-rageous. When I was newly married, I went to the Author's Ball at the Hilton in a party of my husband's grandest business colleagues. Very brown from the South of France, I wore a white strapless dress which was so tight, I didn't need a bra. The five-course dinner was too much for it. As I stood up to dance with one of the directors, it split, leaving me naked to the waist.

OFFICE RELATIONSHIPS

A husband spends far more of his waking life with his secretary, and the people he works with, than with his wife. It is the same for his wife if she goes out to work. It is very easy to get crushes on people you work with. There's natural proximity, there's the charm of the clandestine (we mustn't let anyone in the office know), of working together for a common purpose, and finally, because men basically like to boss, and women to be bossed, there is the fatal charm of the boss/female employee relationship. For if you are used to obeying a man when he says 'take a letter', or 'make me a cup of coffee', you may find it difficult to say no when he says 'come to bed with me'.

Bear in mind before you either pounce, or accept the pounce across the desk, that people aren't nearly so easy to live with as to work with, and you'd probably be bored to death with your boss or secretary if you had to spend twenty-four hours a day with them. It will also make things very awkward later if you go off them, while they still fancy you, or vice versa. You may be forced to leave a job you like.

Be very careful, too, not to let your husband or wife think that you are keen on someone in the office, or they will go through agonies of jealousy during the day, and raise hell every time you are kept late – even if you are working.

HAVING YOUR HUSBAND'S BOSS TO DINNER

The wife should pull out all the culinary stops and look as beautiful as possible.

But don't flirt with your husband's boss too much or you'll have him sending your husband abroad and coming round on his own!

Invite another amusing but socially reliable couple

to meet him. Then when you and your husband have to leave the room to dish up or pour drinks, he won't be left alone to examine the damp patches or the peeling wallpaper.

Give him plenty to drink but not too much, or he may become indiscreet about company politics, regret it the next day and take against your husband.

General marital problems

COMMUNICATION

One of the beauties of marriage is that you always have someone to look after, and to look after you, to share your problems, and to tell – without boasting – when something good happens to you.

It is vital that couples should get into the habit of talking to each other and be interested in each other's activities, be it a game of cricket, an afternoon at the WI, or a day at the office. If you are able to communicate on a daily level, you will find it much easier to discuss things when a major crisis blows up – like a husband losing his job, a sudden sexual impasse, or the television breaking down.

Nothing is more depressing than seeing married couples on holiday or dining together gazing drearily into space with nothing to say to one another – at best it's a shocking example to unmarried people.

I feel strongly that married women should try to set a good example to newlyweds or people about to get married. Nothing is more morale-lowering for the engaged girl than to be taken aside by a couple of bored and cynical married women and told how dreary marriage is, the only solution being infidelity or burying oneself in one's children. Rather in the same way that women who have children often terrorise women who are pregnant for the first time with hair-raising stories of childbirth.

SEPARATION

In long separations from your husband or wife, there are all the problems of loneliness and fidelity. Even short separations – a week or a weekend – have their own difficulties.

When her husband goes away, a wife steels herself not to mind, and although she misses him, unconsciously she builds up other resources. She finds it is rather fun to read a novel until three o'clock in the morning, have time to get the house straight, watch what programmes *she* wants on television, not have to cook and wash, and be able to see all the people she is not allowed to see when her husband is at home.

Gradually, as the time for her husband's return approaches, she gets more and more excited. She plans a special homecoming dinner, she buys a new dress and goes on a twenty-four hour diet so she will look beautiful. In her mind she has a marvellously idealised picture of his homecoming.

And then he arrives – hungover, grubby, exhausted, and if he's been to America or anywhere else where the time is different from ours, he'll be absolutely knackered. He won't want to do anything else but fall into bed and then only to sleep.

The wife is inevitably disappointed – this is no god returning, merely a husband, grumbling about the rings round the bath, bringing not passion and tenderness but a suitcase of dirty shirts.

Similarly, a husband returning to his wife after some time away will find that an ecstatic welcome is often followed by a good deal of sniping and bad temper. The wife will have stored up so much unconscious resentment at being deprived of his presence, that she will take it out on him for a few days.

The only way to cope with après-separation situations is not to get panicky if your wife or husband acts strangely. It doesn't mean they've met someone else, they are just taking a bit of time to adjust to your presence again. In a small way, it's like starting one's marriage over again.

JEALOUSY

Once your life is centred round one person, it is very easy to become obsessively jealous. Try and keep your jealousy in check: it will only cause you suffering, and make things very difficult for your partner.

If you marry a very pretty girl, or a very attractive man, the fact has to be faced that people will still go on finding them attractive.

Give your wife a certain amount of rope, let her go out to lunch with other men, but start kicking up if it becomes a weekly occurrence with the same man. Never let her have drinks in the evening unless it's business or an old friend, and draw the line at breakfast. If you are married to the sort of man who's always humiliating you by running after women at parties, you'll have to grin and bear it. He's probably just testing his sex appeal, like gorillas beat their chests. Before I was married, a girlfriend and I used to divide men into open gazers, or secret doers. You've probably got an open gazer, so thank your lucky stars you're not married to a secret doer.

If you have an ex-wife or an ex-lover, destroy all evidence before you get married again. Nothing is more distressing for a second wife than coming upon wedding photographs of you and your first wife looking idyllically happy.

However much you may want to reminisce about

your exes, keep it to a minimum, and if you ever have to meet any of your wife's or husband's exes, be as nice to them as possible. No one looks attractive when sulking.

BOREDOM

It was not my intention in this book to deal with marriage in relation to children, but I would like to say a brief word about Cabbage-itis, which is my name for the slough of despond a wife goes through when she has two or more very young children to look after. Invariably she's stuck in the country or a part of town where she has few friends, her husband is going out to work every day and meeting interesting people and she isn't, and she feels dull, inadequate and so bored she could scream.

The family budget won't stretch to any new clothes for her, so she feels it is impossible for her to look attractive. On the occasions when friends bring children over for the day, it seems to be all chaos and clamour. She spends days planning a trip to London, which invariably ends in disappointment: her clothes are all wrong, she's worn out after two hours shopping, the girlfriend she meets for lunch can't talk about anything except people she doesn't know, and if she attempts to take the children she's exhausted before she's begun.

She and her husband can't afford to entertain much, but when they are asked out she finds she is so used to saying 'No' and 'Don't' to children all day, she is unable to contribute to the conversation.

If you are going through this stage – and I think it is one of the real danger zones of marriage – remember that it isn't going to go on for ever. The children will grow up, go to school, and you will have acres of free time to go back to work, to take up hobbies, to make new friends. Whatever you do: don't neglect your appearance. Looking pretty isn't new clothes, it's clean hair, a bit of make-up and a welcoming hug when your husband comes home in the evening.

Remember that your husband must always come first, even before the children. In your obsession with your domestic problems, don't forget that he probably isn't having a very easy time either: desperately pushed for money, harassed at work, buffeted back and forth in a train every day, coming home to a drab fractious wife every night.

So don't catalogue your woes; when he arrives in the evening, concentrate on giving him a good time.

Try and go out at least once a week if it's only to the pictures. Try and read a newspaper, or at least listen to the headlines while you're doing the housework, so you won't feel too much out of touch.

If possible find something remunerative to do even if it's only making paper flowers, typing, or framing pictures. Nothing is more depressing than poverty and if you can make the smallest contribution to the family budget it will be a boost to your morale.

Clothes

CLOTHES AND APPEARANCE

'The reason why so few marriages are happy,' said misogynist Swift, 'is because young ladies spend their time in making nets not cages.'

No wife has any right to let herself go to seed after she's married. She bothered enough to look pretty while she was trying to hook her husband, so it's a poor compliment to him if she slackens up immediately after he's hooked.

Remember that the world is full of pretty girls who are not averse to amorous dalliance, and if you want to keep your husband, you'll have to work hard to go on attracting him.

It's a case, of course, of shacking-up *à son goût*. Some men prefer their wives au naturel, others are like the husband who said to me: 'The marvellous thing about old Sue is that she always looks as neat as a new pin. I've never seen her without make-up or slopping around in jeans.'

Exotic clothes

Remember that no man ever went off his wife because he saw a crowd of men round her. So always pull out the stops when you go to parties, or out in the evening, or pick your husband up from the office. It is important to him that other people think you're attractive.

And even if your husband does prefer you without make-up, put some on when you go to a party. You'll have to compete with all those dollies with their false pieces and their three pairs of false eyelashes. Your husband won't be amused if he has to keep leaving the pretty girl he's chatting up to look after you because you've been abandoned.

If a wife wants to jazz up her husband's wardrobe, her best method is to start giving him exotic clothes for his birthday. He'll never go and buy them of his own accord.

It is also up to husbands and wives to take an interest in each other's appearance. Tell your husband when he looks handsome, and even if you are the sort of man who can't tell a discarded false eyelash from a centipede, compliment your wife on her appearance when she buys a new outfit or is dressed up to go out in the evening.

SEWING
Great row potential here.

Shirt buttons always fly off when the man is getting dressed in the morning, or last thing at night when you're both going to bed, so they never get sewn on. Your wife will also plump for Terylene socks and say they are healthier and cheaper, and can be thrown away when they go into holes, to be told by her husband that his mother always darned his woollen ones.

If the wife really can't sew, she should just content herself with sewing on buttons, and send all major repairs to the cleaners, where they can be done for a few shillings.

Holidays

Much of the chapter on honeymoons applies here. People are so grimly determined to enjoy every moment of their holidays that they feel dismayed and cheated if anything goes wrong.

You're probably both exhausted, particularly if you've only been married a short time, and have had all the strain of getting adjusted. You've been planning and looking forward to your holiday for ages, then you arrive at your destination and find you're so unused to doing nothing that it takes you at least a fortnight to unwind. Then it's time to go home again.

There is also the sex problem. Before you were married, holidays were always treated as safaris. The moment you boarded the train at Victoria, the sap started rising, the eye started roving on the lookout for a holiday playmate. After you're married, the hunting instinct dies very hard. As a friend of mine said: 'Taking a married man to the South of France is rather like taking a foxhound to a meet on a lead, and not letting him join in the chase.'

I'm not a believer in retaliation but if your husband does get a crush on another girl on holiday – carrying her beachbag, always ready with a large towel when she comes up from the sea – your best answer rather than sulking is to take to the nearest gigolo. And if there isn't a gigolo to take, comfort yourself with the thought that holiday romances seldom last beyond the holiday.

Going on holiday with friends, of course, is one of the quickest ways of losing them. The most amiable people turn into absolute monsters when they've got too much spare time on their hands.

Everyone will either want to do different things (lying in the sun, sightseeing, diving, pony trekking, or merely getting drunk) or else no one will admit what they want to do, and go round looking martyred:

'What would you like to do today, my darling?'

'Anything *you* like, darling.'

'Oh don't be awkward.'

Particularly avoid going with people who are much richer than you (you'll worry the whole time about spending too much) or poorer than you (or you'll spend your time grumbling about their meanness).

We went to France once in a party of twelve, all great friends. It was a catastrophe. Meals were exactly like being back at school: 'Hands up for salade niçoise.' All the people who could speak French pulled rank on the people who couldn't or didn't dare. All the wives sulked because all the husbands had got crushes on the one single girl, who was sulking because she couldn't hook the one single man. Bad will was absolutely rampant.

I am painting a gloomy picture of holidays, because I think people often feel that if they've had a disastrous holiday their marriage must be on the rocks. 'If we can't get on when we're on holiday,' they say, 'there must be something radically wrong.' Forget it. Cheerful pessimism is the best approach to a holiday, and console yourself that the most disastrous holidays are always the funniest in retrospect.

HOW TO BEHAVE

On holiday there is invariably one who does the planning – booking rooms, tickets, etc. – and one who resists being planned. If you're the resister, cut down on the beefing, whether it's about the lack of soap, coat-hangers, hot water, drawer space, bed space, or amount of garlic in the food. Remember when in Rome . . . and shut up about it.

Don't overdo the sun – holidays are meant for lots

of sex, and you won't feel like it if you wince every time you touch each other. And it's depressing to start peeling like a ticker-tape welcome as soon as you turn brown.

Travel is inclined to broaden the hips as well as the mind. Take a few shifts and larger sized trousers.

Take lots of books and sleeping pills. One often can't sleep in hot countries, and nothing is more depressing than to feel that all of the good of your holiday is being wasted because of insomnia. Take something to settle your stomach, so you won't spend all night thundering to the lavatory like the Gadarene Swine.

Remember you won't be able to buy the Pill, or whatever you use, in a Catholic country. One couple were staying in a villa in Spain, and a particularly greedy guest came down one morning, found their contraceptive paste in the fridge, thought it was some exotic pâté and spread it on his toast for breakfast.

Go somewhere where there's something to do: a casino, the odd night club, boats to sail, etc.

Money should be shared and kept an eye on: nothing wrecks a holiday more than the constant fear that you may run out.

Husbands and wives should do their own packing to avoid endless recriminations about spongebags, razors and cameras left behind.

It's horrible coming home to a dirty untidy house. If you haven't got a daily, pay a chum a couple of quid to come in the day before you get home to give the house a going over.

Don't show slides. Don't bore everyone when you get back with stories of your holiday. My husband refuses to talk about it, and hangs a notice on his office door saying 'yes'.

Sex

BED

Bed/sex/intercourse/making love – call it what you like – is the cornerstone of marriage. If the sex side of a marriage is really good, you seldom hear of it breaking up. If you keep your partner happy in bed, he's unlikely to stray, and if he does he nearly always comes back.

Few people are born geniuses in bed – it is something you learn step by step, like a child learns to talk. The first essential is to be honest with one another. Don't pretend to be going into ecstasies of excitement if you are not, or your partner will automatically assume he is doing the right things to please you, and keep on doing them.

A wife – if she can possibly help it – shouldn't pretend to be having an orgasm if she is not. Although her husband will flop down satisfied beside her afterwards, she will unconsciously build up a resentment both against him for not seeing through the cheat, and against herself for cheating.

Of course it's not vital to have an orgasm every time you go to bed with a man, but the fact remains that it's much nicer if you do. It draws you together, it gives you a marvellous feeling, and it's the best sleeping pill in the world.

Another myth that must be shattered is that men are lustful beasts whose appetites must be slaked, and women have to endure it.

'Your father was very good to me and never bothered me much,' Victorian mothers used to tell daughters who were about to get married. 'Just shut your eyes and think of England.'

Recent research, however, has discovered that

women can be just as highly sexed as men, need intercourse just as often, but in most instances are too inhibited to ask for it.

Nothing that two people do in their own home

A wife should therefore not be ashamed to take a wholehearted enjoyment in sex, ask for it often, and if her husband isn't forthcoming, to seduce him, by making herself pretty, wearing sexy underwear, or simply by wandering round in the nude.

Don't be too fastidious. Nothing that two people who love each other do for their mutual enjoyment in the privacy of their own home can be wrong. If he's on a Lolita kick, pander to his whims and dress up in a gym tunic. If she's got a slave girl complex, tie her up before you make love to her.

Sex books are quite helpful but they always made us howl with laughter. They kept talking about the 'upright male member', which made us think of an incorruptible MP.

Read as much erotic literature as you can get your hands on, not only to excite you, but to give you ideas. Marriage needs every novelty to keep it going. A man I know said his wife was absolutely sensational in bed for at least a month after she'd read *Fanny Hill*.

For beginners (see the chapter on the honeymoon) the thing to remember is to take things slowly. It may be six months or a year before you manage to establish a sexual rapport. It's only in books that the man goes on drilling all night, and suddenly the rock splits and the oil comes gushing out. Enthusiasm is nine-tenths of the battle, and perseverance. Kindness and gratitude are also essential. Tell your husband what doesn't work for you, but make pretty sure you tell him when it is good. If having the inside of your thighs stroked excites you, say so. Don't let him wait thirty years to find out.

On a Lolita kick

Once a year

HOW OFTEN

This is entirely up to you. Everyone lies about it if you ask them. I read in one book that the average man of thirty has sexual intercourse 2.8 times a week. When I told my husband, a rather smug gleam came into his eye, but he was curious to know what they did on the .8 occasion.

On the other hand, one Indian sex manual says that during the first year of marriage couples should have intercourse three times a night for the first three months, twice a night for the next three months, and every night for the rest of the year. After which I suppose you die of exhaustion.

There's no rule. Sometimes you may get a jag and have each other a dozen times in a weekend, sometimes if you're both tired you may not feel like touching each other for a week or so.

HOW NOT TO LOOK IN BED

Curlers and great blobs of face cream are grounds for divorce – no woman need wear them. If you want curly hair, get a set of heated rollers. If you want a soft skin, put on face cream in the bath.

People should wash and clean their teeth before they go to bed, and have at least one bath a day. This may sound elementary, but it's amazing how many people don't, and, sweat fetishists apart, most people would rather make love to someone who smells and tastes good.

Have separate beds if you must, but not separate rooms. Once you get on to the separate rooms kick, it's so easy to shut yourself in every night and grow further and further away from your partner. If one of you snores, or is a bad sleeper and wants to read, have a bed made up in the spare room, so you can slip into it if you get really desperate about three o'clock in the morning.

Don't, however, get out of the habit of making love. Quite often if you've been snapping at each other you will find that once you sleep together everything will be all right again.

I met a girl the other day who boasted she only gives herself to her husband once a year on his birthday. A woman should be grateful that her husband wants her, and any woman who keeps on saying 'I don't feel like it tonight', unless she's ill, pregnant or recovering from a baby, deserves to have an unfaithful husband.

Equally no man should deny his wife, if she obviously wants it. There's no excuse for the sort of career man – an American, as it happens – who will only sleep with his wife on Friday and Saturday, so he'll be fresh for work on the weekdays.

Another of the great myths about sex is that for the

first year you glut yourselves like someone working in a sweet shop, and after that the glamour wears off and you settle down to pastimes like bringing up children and gardening. In any good marriage, sex should get better and better as the years go by, even if you indulge in it marginally less often.

Affaires

Another great fallacy is that marriage stops you falling in love with people. It doesn't. One of the most happily married men I know says he was riddled with guilt because he developed a violent crush on a blonde staying in the same hotel while he was on honeymoon. If you were the sort of person who was always falling in love before marriage, you'll probably go on doing it afterwards. Don't panic – nip it in the bud early. Refuse to see the person concerned. It will tear your guts out for a few weeks, but you'll find you get over it, just as you got over the crushes you had before you were married.

If you fancy someone, and you know they fancy you, don't try and rely on mutual self-control. These things if allowed to develop invariably get out of hand and can escalate into nasty things like divorce. The most shortsighted remark ever made at the beginning of an affaire is: 'You're happily married and I'm happily married, and if we have an affaire, we're both adult enough not to let it get out of hand or anyone get hurt.' This is rubbish. Someone always gets hurt, and it'll probably be you. And remember, once your husband or wife finds out you are having an affaire with someone else it will cause them appalling unhappiness, and your marriage will never be the 'glad confident morning' it was.

MUTUAL INFIDELITY
'Husbands are such a bore,' said a friend of mine. 'They always want to know who you're dating.' Some couples manage to go their own way, making a pledge of mutual infidelity, but I cannot help feeling that one of the partners must be enjoying it more than the other.

If you must have affaires, be discreet. The cardinal sin is to be found out. And when it's all over and you're feeling a louse and you want to clear your conscience, don't indulge in tearful confessions to your husband and feel you've cleaned the slate. It will upset him quite unnecessarily.

DISCOVERY
If you do discover your husband is having an affaire with someone, and he doesn't know you know, play it cool. It may blow over. Remember, 'the robb'd that smiles steals something from the thief.'

If you find out, and your partner knows you know, the only solution is to raise hell, and insist that it stops immediately. Once you start condoning something like this, you're lost. Usually the jolt of your finding out and minding so much is enough to make him give up the other person, in which case welcome him home like the prodigal son, and *never never* reproach him again.

People often have affaires as a bid for more attention from their partners and purposely leave clues so that their partners will find out and be jolted into loving them more. So if you discover your husband is having an affaire with someone, have a look at your own behaviour before you blame him to see if it's you who's at fault.

68

A FEW PRACTICAL SUGGESTIONS

If your wife seems like a bolter, put her on the same passport, then you won't waste a fortune in air tickets getting her back.

If you suspect your partner is having an affaire with a particular person, go into howls of immoderate laughter every time that person's name is mentioned. When they ask why you're laughing, laugh some more and say no one takes that idiot seriously. Nothing douses passion quicker than ridicule. I really fancied a man once, until someone pointed out he looked like Dracula.

DETECTION

There are a number of indications that your partner is having an affaire with someone:

If your husband insists he's been lunching at the local with the boys, and comes home reeking of garlic, gets out a packet of matches with the Mirabelle printed on it, and lights a king-size cigarette when he normally smokes Woodbines.

If he starts a pointless row at breakfast, so he can storm out of the house, and needn't come back until late.

If he suddenly starts working late consistently and comes home smelling of scent.

If he looks happy on a Monday morning, and miserable on a Friday night.

If he suddenly starts having a bath in the morning.

If the distance between the ends of his tie is different in the morning from the evening.

If he keeps making ridiculous excuses to buy more cigarettes during the weekend when there are plenty of packets in the house.

If there's a spate of wrong numbers, it may not be burglars . . .

If your wife after always dressing scruffily for the office suddenly starts smartening herself up, shaving her legs, buying new underwear, and getting home late.

If she doesn't look dismayed when you say you're going to America for three weeks.

If she is home all day and the loo seat is up when you get home.

If she suddenly gets sexually revved up. Women are like machines, the more they're used the better they work.

If she starts suggesting you make love to her standing on your head, she may have been reading the *Kama Sutra*.

If she starts leaving intellectual books by the bed, or tidying the house frantically in the morning . . .

If you have a man friend to stay, and he knows where to put things away when he's doing the drying up.

If you're both out to work and you come home and find the towels all tidy in the bathroom instead of scrumpled up as usual. Or if the cat isn't hungry . . .

If the cat isn't hungry

Coming unstuck

Everyone can make a mistake, and there's no point in a couple sticking together if they're utterly miserable, even for the sake of the children, who would be much happier with one contented parent than two continually at war. Do try and distinguish, however, between a temporary bad patch, which all marriages go through, and a permanent rift. Divorce is very unpleasant and very expensive. A great deal of mudslinging and bitterness will inevitably occur, and there's the nasty business of dividing friends and property.

So before you run off, whether it's with someone or not, make absolutely sure you want to go. Your partner may or may not take you back afterwards, and the longer you stay away the more difficult it will be to start again.

Another thing to remember is that it's very cold outside the matrimonial cage. One beautiful woman I know recently left her husband because she was bored and unhappy. She was back within six months.

When she was safely married, she had a wonderful time, having numerous affaires, being hotly pursued by hordes of men (for nothing is more attractive to a man than a bored, beautiful but safely married woman – all fun and no fear). Once she had left her husband the men who had been swarming round her weren't nearly so anxious to declare themselves, and she soon found it was back to single girl status with all t   h   e nagging worries of who was going to take her out the next night.

Sometimes an affaire can ventilate a marriage and make a couple appreciate each other more:

Another friend of mine became so infatuated with

her lover that she left her husband. Next morning she and her lover went along to the lover's solicitor, who asked her if there was anything detrimental they could use against her husband in the divorce. Was he cruel? Did he neglect her? Did he have affaires with other women or beat her up?

She thought for a minute and then burst into tears, saying she couldn't think of anything wrong with him. She rushed out of the solicitor's office and went back to her husband, whom to her amazement she found absolutely devastated by her departure. They have been happily married ever since.

Breeding

'Has Tom fertilised Wendy yet?' asked one of the small bridesmaids gazing at the bridal couple at a recent wedding.

Premature certainly, but it's amazing how many brides have to carry extra large bouquets these days.

An extra large bouquet

A girl I know who was married when she was eight months pregnant was given a year's subscription to the Nappy Service by her office as a wedding present. Although there will be a few raised eyebrows if a baby turns up before nine months have elapsed, particularly if it is a spanking ten pounder and cannot be fobbed off as premature, the fact remains that the moment you get back from your honeymoon, people will start expecting you to get pregnant.

Every time the wife looks tired, has a bilious attack or leaves a party early, people will start exchanging knowing looks.

If after two years nothing happens, the pressure will really be on. Hints are dropped about 'getting set in your ways', or 'too used to living on two incomes'. People will keep suggesting you move to the country and send you estate agents' lists of bijou residences with large gardens. Dire warnings will be given about the difficulty of having babies after the age of twenty-five.

After three years, you will be offered names of 'perfectly marvellous gynaecologists', and friends will say the wife is overtiring herself and ought to give up work. People will take her aside and say: 'Don't you think Henry ought to see a doctor as well, darling?'

Parents-in-law will display angst about not having any grandchildren to talk about at bridge parties.

They should all realise that it's none of their business. Anyone who starts interfering on this subject deserves a flea in their ear.

If couples don't have children, it's either because they don't want to yet, or because they're trying and they can't. Not being able to have children, whether it's temporary or permanent, is extremely distressing. (There is something tragic and yet ridiculous about those abortive threshings night after night.) Outsiders should not contribute to this distress by asking stupid questions.

I couldn't have children and, after seven traumatic years of trailing from doctor to doctor, we finally in extreme trepidation adopted one. It has been an unqualified success. Within twenty-four hours of the child's arrival we were infatuated with him, and couldn't imagine life without him.

Everyone told us we were too set in our ways. You lead such a full life, they said. Too full? Too empty? Too full perhaps of empty things. Children are not nearly so much work as alarmist mothers crack them up to be, and they are more fun than one could believe possible.

One of the great revelations of my life was how immeasurably much better life was when one was married than unmarried. Another was how much better marriage is when one has children.

Conclusion

I am fully aware of the inadequacies of this book. Some aspects of marriage are covered very scantily and some not at all, and because I was writing about staying married, I have dwelt more on the pitfalls than on the very considerable joys of marriage.

'For everyone, and particularly for women and children,' Cecil King wrote recently, 'the essential basis for security and happiness is a loving home.'

Marriage is not a battlefield, it is a partnership, and married people should be partners not rivals. And although it is important to be a reliable wage earner, a splendid cook, a good manager, and magnificent in bed, the most priceless gift one married person can give to another is a merry and a loving heart.

TRANSWORLD PUBLISHERS
61–63 Uxbridge Road, London W5 5SA
www.penguin.co.uk

Transworld is part of the Penguin Random House group of companies
whose addresses can be found at global.penguinrandomhouse.com

First published in Great Britain in 1969 by Methuen & Co Ltd
Mandarin Paperbacks edition published 1988

This updated edition published in 2011 by Bantam Press
an imprint of Transworld Publishers

A CIP catalogue record for this book
is available from the British Library.

ISBN 9781787631434 (cased)

Typeset in 9.25/11.75pt Plantin by Falcon Oast Graphic Art Ltd.
Printed and bound in Great Britain by Clays Ltd, Elcograf S.p.A.

Penguin Random House is committed to a sustainable
future for our business, our readers and our planet. This book is
made from Forest Stewardship Council® certified paper.

1 3 5 7 9 10 8 6 4 2

By Jilly Cooper

FICTION	Riders
	Rivals
	Polo
	The Man Who Made Husbands Jealous
	Appassionata
	Score!
	Pandora
	Wicked!
	Jump!
	Mount!
NON-FICTION	Animals in War
	Class
	How to Survive Christmas
	Hotfoot to Zabriskie Point (with Patrick Lichfield)
	Intelligent and Loyal
	Jolly Marsupial
	Jolly Super
	Jolly Superlative
	Jolly Super Too
	Super Cooper
	Super Jilly
	Men and Supermen
	Women and Supermen
	The Common Years
	Turn Right at the Spotted Dog
	How to Stay Married
	How to Survive from Nine to Five
	Angels Rush In
	Araminta's Wedding
CHILDREN'S BOOKS	Little Mabel
	Little Mabel's Great Escape
	Little Mabel Saves the Day
	Little Mabel Wins
ROMANCE	Bella
	Emily
	Harriet
	Imogen
	Lisa & Co
	Octavia
	Prudence
ANTHOLOGIES	The British in Love
	Violets and Vinegar

Jilly Cooper is a journalist, author and media superstar. The author of many number one bestselling novels, she lives in Gloucestershire with her rescue racing greyhound, Bluebell.

She has been awarded honorary doctorates by the Universities of Gloucestershire and Anglia Ruskin and appointed CBE in 2018 for services to literature and charity.

How to Stay Married, originally published in 1969, was her very first book. Jilly was married to Leo Cooper for fifty-two years, until his death in 2013.